# The Greater Working Woman Devotional

## VOLUME 1

Chantea M. Williams

The Greater Working Woman Devotional, Volume 1
Copyright © 2015 Chantea M. Williams

All rights reserved. No part of this book may be reproduced or used in any form by any means electronic or mechanical, including photocopying, recordings, or information storage and retrieval systems without written permission of the author except for the use of brief quotations in a book review.

Requests for permission to quote from this book must be by email at info@gwwministry.com

Published by Chantea M. Williams
Printed in USA

First Printing, 2015

Unless otherwise noted, scripture quotations are taken from the Holy Bible, New Living Translation copyright ©1996, 2004, 2007, 2013 by Tyndale House Foundation. Used by permission of Tyndale House Publishers, Inc., Carol Stream, Illinois 60188. All rights reserved.

ISBN-13: 978-1507860229
ISBN-10: 1507860226

# DEDICATION

*This book is dedicated to all the women who are trying to become greater one day at a time. Don't give up on life nor abandon your God-given dreams. He still wants to use an imperfect you for His perfect will.*

# PHILIPPIANS 1:6

*And I am certain that God, who began the good work within you, will continue his work until it is finally finished on the day when Christ Jesus returns.*

# CONTENTS

DEDICATION .......................................................................... iii
ACKNOWLEDGMENTS ........................................................ vi
INTRODUCTION ...................................................................... 1
DAY 1 ......................................................................................... 3
DAY 2 ......................................................................................... 5
DAY 3 ......................................................................................... 7
DAY 4 ......................................................................................... 9
DAY 5 ....................................................................................... 11
DAY 6 ....................................................................................... 13
DAY 7 ....................................................................................... 16
DAY 8 ....................................................................................... 18
DAY 9 ....................................................................................... 20
DAY 10 ..................................................................................... 22
DAY 11 ..................................................................................... 24
DAY 12 ..................................................................................... 26
DAY 13 ..................................................................................... 28
DAY 14 ..................................................................................... 30
DAY 15 ..................................................................................... 32
DAY 16 ..................................................................................... 34
DAY 17 ..................................................................................... 36
DAY 18 ..................................................................................... 38
DAY 19 ..................................................................................... 40
DAY 20 ..................................................................................... 42

DAY 21 .................................................................. 45
DAY 22 .................................................................. 47
DAY 23 .................................................................. 49
DAY 24 .................................................................. 51
DAY 25 .................................................................. 53
DAY 26 .................................................................. 55
DAY 27 .................................................................. 57
DAY 28 .................................................................. 59
DAY 29 .................................................................. 61
DAY 30 .................................................................. 63
ABOUT THE AUTHOR ..................................... 66

# ACKNOWLEDGMENTS

To God be the glory in all things, especially His patience with me in walking in total obedience. I want to thank all the women who have allowed me to encourage them with daily email devotionals over the years. It keeps me on the right track. I appreciate all the men and women of God who have poured into me over the years so that I can be who God called me to be. I will forever be indebted to all of you. A special thank you to my editor Michelle Cameron, who made my dreams come true!

# INTRODUCTION

This is a devotional book for women from all walks of life for encouragement. This book is not for perfect women but only for the flawed ones. Whether you are a teen mother struggling to overcome obstacles in life, a woman in corporate America trying to make her mark in this world or just a woman looking for a little encouragement, this book is for you!

Women function simultaneously in different roles every day. We sometimes get bogged down with meetings, everyone's expectations and caring for those who are near and dear to our hearts. With our may obligations we often forget our worth, so our actions lead us to getting discouraged and wanting to give up and just throw in the towel.

These inspirational messages will prayerfully encourage, empower and equip you to be that Greater Working Woman! Jeremiah 29:11 (NIV) states, "For I know the plans I have for you," declares the Lord, "plans to prosper you and not to harm you, plans to give you hope and a future." We don't have to worry about what our future holds if we leave it in God's hands! He will supply all of our needs according to His riches in glory. (Philippians 4:19) You can sleep at night knowing that God is in control. He gave the life of His Son so that we can have an abundant life.

Dry those weeping eyes, pick your head up and walk tall knowing that everything will work out for your good! Although the results may not be the way you want them, you must believe that God's way is the only way. Start living like the favor of God is working in your life.

So, Greater Working Woman, walk in your Kingdom authority and know that as long as you delight yourself in Him, then He will give you the desires of your heart (Psalm 37:4).

# DAY 1

## His Plans For You
## Jeremiah 29:11

**For I know the plans I have for you," says the Lord. "They are plans for good and not for disaster, to give you a future and a hope.**

Our society today has influenced people to choose the get-rich schemes because it's the shortest path to success. The Lord already declares that He has plans to prosper us! So why are we looking for the fly-by-night deals? All He requires of us is to surrender all things to Him. Not some things, but ALL things. Our hope and future lies in the Almighty!

We have to stop looking with our natural eyes and open our spiritual eyes to see just how beautiful our life really is. Let's stop trying to keep up with what the world says is "blessed" and truly enjoy the blessings of God. It's those little things that matter the most. I challenge you to start a thank you journal. Each day write down one thing that you are thankful for and the only rule is that you cannot write the same thing twice. It won't take long to notice just how prosperous we are.

## Prayer

Father, I know Your plans to prosper me are better than any plan I could ever come up with on my own. This year I will obey Your plans for my life. My obedience shall bring spiritual growth and an overflow of blessings. I declare that doors shall be opened that no man can shut and that You will close doors that no man can open. I am expecting my future to be greater than my past. In Jesus' name, amen!

# DAY 2

## I'm Lost Without You

## Psalm 119:59

**I pondered the direction of my life, and I turned to follow your statutes.**

Have you ever had that lost feeling? When we are in a store and a child wanders off out of our sight, we frantically look for them until they are safe in our arms. When we lose jobs, we go searching for new ones so that we can provide for our families. What do we do when we are spiritually lost? What do we do when a loved one is spiritually lost? Do we even recognize that we or they are lost? Do we put enough attention on our spiritual well-being as we do on other areas of our life?

God doesn't expect us to have a Bible in our hand every second of the day with the appearance of looking holy. Instead, He wants us to hide His word in our heart. No matter how much knowledge or education we may obtain in this world, nothing matters if we do not have Him. Having God in our lives makes us women of worth!

## Prayer

Father, I am lost without You! I know that I have allowed the busyness of life to distract me away from You, but I shall allow the help of the Holy Spirit to make sure I grow more spiritually this year than last year. I have pondered the direction of my life, and I turned to follow your laws. I want You to direct every area of my life. In Jesus' name, amen!

# DAY 3

## A Fresh Wind

## Acts 2:2

**Suddenly, there was a sound from heaven like the roaring of a mighty windstorm in the skies above them, and it filled the house where they were meeting.**

This is your year! Your identity will be confirmed this year. Your purpose will be clearer this year. You will be restored this year. You will be revived this year. You will be released from people this year. You will be more confident this year. This is the year where you will not only see God turning things around in your favor, but you will feel it on the inside. This year you will walk in more boldness for Him. This year your faith will be tested more but you are already a conqueror through Christ Jesus.

You shall not walk in fear this year. This is your year! The year where you will feel a Fresh Wind consume you and touch every area of your life! I urge you to get in the wind and witness the power of God work like never before in your life. What does that mean? You are going to have to study the word more. You are going to have pray more, and yes, you will have to fast more. You are going to have to step out of your comfort zone without fear of what others may say or do. Stop allowing your past to be your hindrance. None of us are worthy but that didn't stop Him from loving us. Rahab had a past, but God. The woman at the well had a past, but God. Abigail was married to a foolish man, but God. You cannot allow another year to pass with minimal results. No! This year you must make Him your choice. This year we are breaking all the rules. So, woman of God what is it going to be.... the same old thing, or are you going to receive your Fresh Wind?

## Prayer

Father, I need a fresh wind from Heaven. A fresh wind to touch my mind so that my thoughts are not the same; a fresh wind to touch my mouth so that my conversations are not the same. I shall read Your word more this year. I shall fast and pray more this year. I shall get more involved in ministry this year. I shall be transformed for the glory of God this year. Satan, get behind me because I'm getting in this Fresh Wind. The Holy Spirit is doing a new thing in me this year. Old things are passed away and all things have become new. Chains are being broken in my life this year. Strongholds are being released in my life this year. Victory is already mine this year. I speak a Fresh Wind into my life this year. In Jesus' name, amen!

# DAY 4

## You Can Have A New Beginning

## Zechariah 3:3-4

3 Jeshua's clothing was filthy as he stood there before the angel. 4 So the angel said to the others standing there, "Take off his filthy clothes." And turning to Jeshua he said, "See, I have taken away your sins, and now I am giving you these fine new clothes."

When I read these verses, they remind me of how we must look in all of our filth. Thank God that the blood of Jesus has taken our sins away. People may never allow you to get over your past in their eyes, but don't let their problem become your problem. When you have been washed in the blood, old things pass away and all things become new. So many times we allow our past to hinder our future because of fear.

It's okay to be concerned about the opinion of others, but when you allow those opinions to dictate your life then you have created a problem for yourself that you will never be able to solve. The key thing to remember is that their opinion does not have to become your reality. Think about that for a minute. It only becomes your truth if you start to live by it.

Isn't it glorious to know that when God sees us, He sees what we can become and not what we settle for? He sees the best in us continuously and He is just waiting for us to see the same thing. No man will ever be perfect on this earth again; that's why Jesus died. He redeemed us back to our original state but we have to recognize it, believe it, live it, walk it, breathe it and claim it. We are all as filthy rags and fall of short of His glory daily, but thank God for His Son. Put on your new clothes of royalty and let us be all who God created us to be! After all, the life we live is a direct representation of who we think He is.

## Prayer

Father, I want to put on this new wardrobe that You have given me. I shall walk tall and hold my head up high. The sinful life I used to live, I don't want to live it anymore. I want to be made anew and refreshed. I want to be revived. I want to be restored. I want to be made over. I am not what people see. I am what You see. Father, clean this house from the inside out. I declare my new beginning today. In Jesus' name, amen!

# DAY 5

## Expect It To Happen
## Psalm 5:3

**Listen to my voice in the morning, Lord. Each morning I bring my requests to you and wait expectantly.**

When you pray do you expect God to answer you long after you come up off your knees? Do you still believe, long after you come down from your spiritual high? It's easy to believe as the words are coming out of our mouths but do you still believe 3 months later when you are still waiting on your answer? As believers we are to wait and expect God to move in our situations. He delights when His children come to Him with their cares. The Bible tells us in Hebrews 4:16 (KJV) to come boldly before the throne of grace. He wants to move on our behalf but we must have the faith to go along with it. Just as an earthly father finds joy in helping his children, our Heavenly Father enjoys the same opportunity.

He can do more for us than any man can do. Our waiting is not being idle. We must still live as though what we asked for has already been given. What are you waiting for? Go ahead and tell your Daddy what you need. He's waiting on you to talk to Him.

## Prayer

Father, I come to You, expecting You to answer! Father, I come expecting You to move on my behalf and for those that I'm praying for. I expect You to heal and deliver. I expect You to work miracles. I expect You to make a way out of no way. I expect You to provide for my needs. I expect You to watch over my family. I release my faith and believe without a shadow of a doubt that You will honor Your word. You are the same God yesterday, today and forever more. You said if I seek You first and Your righteousness then all things will be added unto me. In Jesus' name, amen!

# DAY 6

## Overcoming a Jonah Mentality
## Jonah 4:1-4

**This change of plans greatly upset Jonah, and he became very angry. ² So he complained to the Lord about it: "Didn't I say before I left home that you would do this, Lord? That is why I ran away to Tarshish! I knew that you are a gracious and compassionate God, slow to get angry and filled with unfailing love. I knew how easily you could cancel your plans for destroying these people. ³ Just kill me now, Lord! I'd rather be dead than alive because nothing I predicted is going to happen." ⁴ The Lord replied, "Is it right for you to be angry about this?"**

Jonah didn't want to preach God's word to his enemies because he knew just how gracious and forgiving his God was. He knew that if they repented then God would not destroy them. We often do the same thing knowing and unknowingly. We want our enemies to suffer even more than what they caused upon us. We want them to really "get it" from God so they will know that they were wrong.

If we have the same mindset as our enemies, then are we

really any better than they are? If we wish the same calamity or worse over them, is that Christ like? Who are we to get angry when God forgives them? Who are we to get mad when God gives them another chance? How many chances has God given you? It's easy to say, "I'll get you for getting me" but it's even better to say, "I'll pray for you even though you got me."

It's a growth process to get to this point but it's a place where all Christians should want to be. When we get in God's word, we will have peace, even with our enemies. Don't you know the best revenge for your enemy is for the people who harmed you to come into a relationship with Christ? Your only real enemy is the devil.

The word tells us in Ephesians that this is spiritual warfare. "For our struggle is not against flesh and blood, but against the rulers, against the authorities, against the powers of this dark world and against the spiritual forces of evil in the heavenly realms" (Ephesians 6:12). This fight can only be fought in the Spirit. Let us all take the necessary steps to overcome a Jonah mentality. After all, God has the final say and there is nothing we can do about it!

## Prayer

Father, forgive me for the times I wanted my enemies to suffer like they made me suffer rather than praying for their soul. Father, forgive me for having a Jonah mentality. Forgive me for not wanting Your grace and mercy extended to those who cause harm to Your children. The truth is they need Your grace and mercy just as much as I do. Today I lift up every enemy the devil has turned on me and I pray that You will touch their hearts in a special way. I pray that they will turn from their wicked ways and repent. I pray that they will acknowledge You and know You in the pardon of their sins. I pray that they will be saved, sanctified and filled with the Holy Ghost. Father, don't allow them to die in their sins. I pray that they will confess You as their Lord and Saviour. Soften their hearts to hear from You through whatever means You may use to get their attention. If You are sending me as the mouthpiece then I shall obey without hesitation. I shall overcome evil with good and You shall get the glory through me! In Jesus' mighty and wonderful name I pray, amen!

# DAY 7

## Giving Up Is Never An Option
## Job 8:5-7

**⁵ But if you pray to God and seek the favor of the Almighty, ⁶ if you are pure and live with complete integrity, he will surely rise up and restore your happy home. ⁷ And though you started with little, you will end with much.**

Don't allow small defeats in areas where you are struggling to be your end. As long as we are alive and well, we have time to get it together. Don't give up so soon. You have yet to experience the greatness of God working in your life. He still longs to show you favor and His goodness. He is still waiting on you. He hasn't given up on you, so don't give up on yourself. You must keep holding on because all you need is faith that is the size of a mustard seed to move mountains. God is not expecting you to do it in your own strength. He wants you to trust Him like never before. He is willing, ready and able to move those mountains, but He is waiting on you to just ask Him. We may have to ask for a period of time before we see change, but remember that we walk by faith and not by sight.

## Prayer

Father, I am not going to give up. You have brought me too far to turn back now. I shall seek You earnestly day and night. I will not give up anymore. I am an overcomer. I am a winner. I am more than a conqueror. I am because He is! My faith shall cause God to move on my behalf. In Jesus' name, amen!

# DAY 8

## When the Spirit Speaks
## Acts 13:2

**One day as these men were worshiping the Lord and fasting, the Holy Spirit said, "Dedicate Barnabas and Saul for the special work I have for them."**

Is anyone waiting for an answer from the Lord? Has anyone been dealing with a situation for a while and still haven't heard a word from Heaven? Are you just praying or are you worshiping and fasting along with your prayers? Sometimes God wants more from us than just a prayer request. He desires all of us. He just doesn't want us to give Him a to-do list but He wants us to spend time with Him. While these men were in the midst of worshiping and fasting to the Lord, the Holy Spirit spoke to them and gave clear instructions. When was the last time you received clear instructions from the Lord? Have you done a fast lately? When we fast, we are removing things that could distract us from hearing God's voice and replacing that time with reading and meditating on God's word or just worshiping. I encourage you to try it.

## Prayer

Father, I need the Holy Spirit to speak to me. As I fast and worship, prepare me to hear Your voice clearly. Father, open my ears and my heart to receive from You like never before. I know that just one word from You can change my situation around. Speak Lord, for Your servant is listening. In Jesus' name, amen!

# DAY 9

## Stop Looking For The Loud Voice
## 1 Kings 19:11-13

11 "Go out and stand before me on the mountain," the Lord told him. And as Elijah stood there, the Lord passed by, and a mighty windstorm hit the mountain. It was such a terrible blast that the rocks were torn loose, but the Lord was not in the wind. After the wind there was an earthquake, but the Lord was not in the earthquake. 12 And after the earthquake there was a fire, but the Lord was not in the fire. And after the fire there was the sound of a gentle whisper. 13 When Elijah heard it, he wrapped his face in his cloak and went out and stood at the entrance of the cave. And a voice said, "What are you doing here, Elijah?"

Why do we always look for God to talk to us in a loud voice? We need lightening to flash with a loud boom before we believe that God is talking to us. Why is that? Do we really want to hear from God or do we want to hear what we want to hear? There is a difference. There will be times where God's voice is loud and clear. There will also be times when God's voice is just a whisper. Will you listen to the whisper?

Will you recognize the whisper? Will you obey the whisper? God's voice is the same no matter what volume it is in. God's instructions are the same no matter how He relays it to us.

God can speak through His creation just as profoundly and powerful as a human being. When was the last time you enjoyed nature and looked for God to speak to you through it? Don't limit yourself on how you hear from God. Just make sure that you can hear Him no matter how He speaks!

## Prayer

Father, I thank You for speaking to me in many different ways depending on the situation. You are not restricted to only one form of communication. Help me to slow down enough to recognize every time You speak to me. I cannot afford to miss one word from You. In Jesus' name, amen!

# DAY 10

## Can You Hear Me Now?

## Jeremiah 35:17

**"Therefore, Lord God Almighty, the God of Israel, says: 'Because you refuse to listen or answer when I call, I will send upon Judah and Jerusalem all the disasters I have threatened."**

Listening seems to be a lost skill in today's society. Everyone has something to say and everyone wants to speak at the same time. Fear of not being heard has made us deaf to the voice of God. We get so busy making plans and meeting deadlines that we don't even hear the Holy Spirit when He is whispering in our ears. What makes us so busy that we don't listen? Have we forgotten how to listen? When was the last time you just sat and listened to God? When was the last time you went outside and just listened to the sounds of nature created by God? Some of you may be saying to yourselves, I have never done that before while others can't remember the last time they did those things. Instead of being ready to give our two cents before the conversation has barely started, let's listen more. The book of James reminds us that we should be slow to speak but quick to listen (James 1:19).

## Prayer

Father, I admit that I don't always take time to listen to what You have to say. Sometimes I allow myself to get so busy that I forget to listen to the Holy Spirit talking to me. Help me to be a more active listener. Help me to listen to You more attentively in my prayer and meditation time with You. I need to hear You more clearly in my life in every area so that I can make wise choices. I don't want to drown out Your voice with the noise and busyness of life. I want to slow down long enough to hear You speaking clearly to me. Father, prepare my ears and heart to receive from You today like never before. I thank You for the gift of listening. In Jesus' name, amen!

# DAY 11

## We Have To Run Our Own Race
## Hebrews 12:1

**Therefore, since we are surrounded by such a huge crowd of witnesses to the life of faith, let us strip off every weight that slows us down, especially the sin that so easily hinders our progress. And let us run with endurance the race God has set before us.**

Have you ever seen a cross country runner try to do the pole vault? Have you ever seen a hockey player try to play football in his hockey gear? Have you ever seen a ballerina play basketball in her leotard and tutu? You would probably think these people were crazy trying to do something that they are not trained to do. That can be the same with us at times. Sometimes the weight that we carry slows us down because we are trying to run someone else's race. We cannot compare our gifts and talents to the next person.

As women we are constantly comparing ourselves to each other and in the process we tear each other down. That should not be so. We should be lifting up each other and encouraging one another. We should be rejoicing with our sisters when they are blessed and have compassion when they are going through difficult times. Our end goal, Heaven, is the same but how we each get there is a different testimony for everyone. Let's resolve to stop comparing ourselves and run the race with the endurance that God has set before us.

## Prayer

Father, I thank You for my race that is set before me. Help me to encourage and lift up my sisters in Christ. I shall not spend another moment comparing myself to someone else. Lord, I need strength to endure to the end on my path. I shall run my own race. In Jesus' name, amen!

# DAY 12

## My Eyes Have Been Opened
## Psalm 119:18

**Open my eyes to see the wonderful truths in your law.**

Have you ever been blinded by your own biases? Have you ever seen only what you wanted to see? Have you ever refused to see the truth even though it was staring you right in the face? What makes us blind to the truth anyway? It's only another attack from the enemy. If he can keep us blind, then we can't see our way. I'm referring to a spiritual blindness.

That's why the scripture says we walk by faith and not by sight (2 Corinthians 5:7). What we see in the natural is limited to the strength of our eyes. I don't know about you but my natural vision hasn't been 20/20 for quite some time now so I cannot depend on my own eyes to give me the whole truth. In the same way we desire 20/20 vision, it's important that our spiritual vision remain as clear as possible.

That clarity can only come through the power of the Holy Spirit. The more we read God's word, spend time in His presence and spend time praying and fasting, our vision will become clearer.

God desires for our spiritual awareness to be on point not only for our lives and those we love, but more importantly, for the ones whom He brings in our path on a daily basis. We never know when God will give us a word to speak to someone while in the grocery store or sitting in the salon or to a coworker. God can't give it to us if we remain blinded spiritually. Think about it. What are you seeing today? Are you able to see clearly? If you are not satisfied then resolve to make the necessary changes today. God is still waiting.

## Prayer

Father, open my eyes to see the wonderful truths in Your instruction. Open my eyes every time I read Your word so that I can really see what I need to see and not what I want to see. Open the eyes of my heart so that I can recognize the truth and depart from evil. Open the eyes of my spirit to see when the enemy is at work and when the Holy Spirit is at work. I see the need to be able to have a clear vision in order to run my race more effectively. In Jesus' name, amen!

# DAY 13

## A Woman of Wisdom

## Proverbs 3:13-18

**13 Happy is the person who finds wisdom and gains understanding. 14 For the profit of wisdom is better than silver, and her wages are better than gold. 15 Wisdom is more precious than rubies; nothing you desire can compare with her. 16 She offers you light in her right hand, and riches and honor in her left. 17 She will guide you down delightful paths; all her ways are satisfying. 18 Wisdom is a tree of life to those who embrace her; happy are those who hold her tightly.**

I think sometimes we take having wisdom for granted. Wisdom is often underappreciated until we are in the middle of a trial. It's at that moment we recognize that wisdom would have kept us from some of the things that we have to endure. As greater working women, it is vital that we seek godly wisdom not **just** for ourselves but for those who we will encourage and **pray for** in their time of need. Wisdom will guide us, keep our mouths closed and tell us that silence at times is the best option. Wisdom is one of the most priceless jewels but is the least sought after. When we look back over our lives, we can automatically see where wisdom would have changed the outcome of certain situations. We can look at people we know and don't know and say, "if they only had wisdom, they would be so much better off." Why is it that we disregard wisdom? Why do we just throw it aside as if we know all the answers? Wisdom is a tree of life to those who embrace her. Let us strive this year to truly be women of wisdom!

## Prayer

Father, help me to be a wise woman in all that I do, not just for my own benefit but for the benefit of others. I want to be able to give sound advice to a friend in need or to a neighborhood child. I come to You now asking for wisdom in the same manner that King Solomon did long ago. Spirit of the most wise God, fill me with godly wisdom. I need to be able to discern between good and evil all the days of my life. In Jesus' name, amen!

# DAY 14

## Can You Hear Greater?
## Exodus 6:6-9

6 "Therefore, say to the people of Israel: 'I am the Lord. I will free you from your oppression and will rescue you from your slavery in Egypt. I will redeem you with a powerful arm and great acts of judgment. 7 I will claim you as my own people, and I will be your God. Then you will know that I am the Lord your God who has freed you from your oppression in Egypt. 8 I will bring you into the land I swore to give to Abraham, Isaac, and Jacob. I will give it to you as your very own possession. I am the Lord!'" 9 So Moses told the people of Israel what the Lord had said, but they refused to listen anymore. They had become too discouraged by the brutality of their slavery.

The children of Israel had already been in slavery over 400 years. It was hard for them to except anything else that didn't look like slavery. It was hard for them to hear anything else except for the day's tasks. Even though they were God's chosen people and destined for greater, they allowed slavery to blind them from God's reality of their lives. Sounds a little like us, don't you think?

Sometimes the things that we go through hurt us so badly that it blocks the word of the Lord from being received in our hearts. There are times when we are caught off guard and shaken and if the truth be told the last thing we want to hear is a word from the Lord. I know that you have never been there but I have plenty of times until I got to the point where I pushed past my pain and positioned myself to hear clearly from Him. It was then, and only then, did I receive my breakthrough. No matter how long we have been where we are it still only takes one word from God to change our whole life around.

You have to ask yourself these questions: Is my pain bigger than a word from the Lord? Can I afford to miss out on what God has to say about my situation? Can I do anything to make my situation better without the help of the Lord?

## Prayer

Father, I thank you that I am learning to hear You no matter what state I am in. There is no trial big enough to make me deaf to Your word. I position myself to hear from You right now. In the powerful name of Jesus, amen!

# DAY 15

## You Can't Do It By Yourself
## Jeremiah 17:5

**This is what the LORD says:
"Cursed are those who put their trust in mere humans, who rely on human strength and turn their hearts away from the LORD."**

Read these words out loud. We are superwomen! We are independent! We are strong! We are survivors! We are intelligent! We are beautiful! We are resilient! We are phenomenal! We are fabulous! We have mastered multitasking! In all that we are, we still cannot do it by ourselves! We cannot trust in our own ability. We cannot trust in our own strength.

No matter how long you have been "holding it down" you still cannot do it alone. We have to rely only on the strength of the Lord. His strength will never fail us. His strength will never give out. He can carry all of our burdens in the palm of His hand. Some things that we are carrying, we were never to touch. Some things we are carrying, we were not created to do. We are carrying some things because we are afraid that if we don't do it, then it won't get done.

Let's analyze our lives and take inventory on where we are

trying to carry too much. Then let us pray to God for guidance on how to remove it. After all we only have one life to live and God wants us to enjoy it to the fullest! Your enjoyment may be different from the next woman but the key is to ENJOY LIFE as God allows you.

## Prayer

Father, I admit that sometimes I depend on my own strength. Sometimes I trust myself to get things accomplished. Sometimes I take on more than You ever intended me to do. Father, my fears have crept in and influenced me to do these things but I now know that this is not Your will. Lord, please forgive me. I see now that I would be less stressed if I would just turn it over to You completely and let You handle it in Your perfect wisdom. Your word says to cast all my cares on You because You care for me (1 Peter 5:7). Today, I make a life declaration that I will no longer depend on myself or others but I will solely depend on You. Holy Spirit, reveal to me the areas in my life where I am struggling and help me to release those areas unto the Father. I can't do it by myself. I don't want to do it by myself. Lord, I give You the reins of my life and gladly sit in the passenger seat as You lead. In Jesus' name, amen!

# DAY 16

## Your Heart Speaks Loud and Clear
### Matthew 12:34-35

**34 ... for out of the abundance of the heart the mouth speaketh. ³⁵ A good man out of the good treasure of the heart bringeth forth good things; and an evil man out of the evil treasure bringeth forth evil things.**

Has anyone ever said to you "I know what you mean" and you are thinking, "no you don't because I haven't told you?" Is it possible that we told them everything they needed to know with our actions or the lack there of? The old cliché "your actions speak louder than your words" becomes clearer to me daily. Not only in others but more importantly to myself.

Whatever we value is what we will spend time doing! Whatever we desire is what we will make time to do or spend time doing. I'm sure we all have witnessed someone promise the stars above and in the back of our mind we said "yeah right". Why? Their actions never line up with their words. They talk a good talk but there is no good evidence of a positive change.

If we take a look at our own lives, will our words mirror our actions? Did y'all hear that? I just screamed, "Ouch!" Let us be more cautious this year of the words that come out of our mouth. Let's be more of action this year and less talking. Let's be more patient this year and think about our words before sputtering them out. Let's be more purposeful this year, especially with our words. Let's say what we mean and mean what we say.

## Prayer

Father, help my words to line up with my actions and help my actions to line up with You. I don't want to be known as that woman who talked a lot but did very little. I want to be that woman who has good treasures of my heart which brings forth good things. I want my words to speak life and blessings over any situation. I want my words to make a positive impact on those that will hear them. I ask that the Holy Spirit will take over my words even now. I surrender my mouth and words to You now. Fresh Wind, have Your way with my tongue. I will no longer speak idle words but my words will have power to change things. In Jesus' name, amen!

# DAY 17

## Have You Been Delivered From Your Egypt?
## Exodus 29:46

**and they will know that I am the Lord their God. I am the one who brought them out of the land of Egypt so that I could live among them. I am the Lord their God.**

Egypt for the Israelites meant bondage and slavery. They were at a place where they were not able to fulfill the purpose God had for them. They were stuck doing the same thing day in and day out. They cried out to God and He heard them. He sent Moses as their deliverer and brought them out of Egypt with more than what they went in with!

Do you have an Egypt mentality? What things represent Egypt in your life? What or who has you living in bondage? What does the enemy have his grip on and won't let go? You don't have to stay in bondage. You don't have to be enslaved by sin. You can put a halt to the work of the enemy through the power of the Holy Spirit. Jesus came to deliver us from sin. He paid it all on the cross!

Make a choice to transform your mind according to the word of God. Start thinking positively about yourself and your situations. It's not over until God says so. He has the last word. It doesn't matter what it looks like in the natural, He has the last say so. It doesn't matter what the doctor's report says, He has the last say. It doesn't matter how your credit report may look, He has the last say. It doesn't matter how much is in the bank, He has the last say. It doesn't matter that your enemies seem to encamp all around you, He has the last say. It doesn't matter where you come from, He has the last say. It doesn't matter what the judge says, He has the last say!

## Prayer

Father, I thank You that You have the last say in my life. I choose not to have an Egypt mentality. I choose not to stay in bondage to anyone or anything. You have already freed me. Holy Spirit, help me to walk in that freedom and power. In Jesus' name, amen!

# DAY 18

## It's Pruning Time
## John 15:1-2

**15 "I am the true vine, and my Father is the gardener. 2 He cuts off every branch of mine that doesn't produce fruit, and he prunes the branches that do bear fruit so they will produce even more.**

A lot of times we are carrying a lot of dead weight. Lifeless things have no value. We carry around past hurt, failures or the fear of facing them in the future. We are this beautiful woman but sometimes our beauty is covered up by the all the "dead stuff" around us and in us. It sometimes seems easier to carry the "dead stuff" around than to prune it off so that the new growth can spring forth.

What are you still carrying around that has become a hindrance in your life? If you are not sure, then just ask your closest friends. You might be surprised to hear what they have to say. Sometimes we have been carrying it around so long that it becomes an accessory in our life but it doesn't accessorize who we really are.

Prune in the English dictionary means to trim by cutting away dead or overgrown branches or stems, especially to increase fruitfulness and growth. Did you read that last part? TO INCREASE FRUITFULNESS AND GROWTH. It's pruning time! Let's make a more active effort to prune our lives so that we can be fruitful and grow to what God has already planned for us.

## Prayer

Father, I sometimes carry around dead weight in my life. My fears have had the best of me at times but today I am making a more conscious effort to prune my life. I want to be fruitful and grow. Holy Spirit, please show me the areas in my life that need pruning and help me to tackle them one at a time. I don't want anything in my life that is dead and not adding value. You have too much in store for me not to truly enjoy life. As I make this new commitment, lead and guide me all the way. In Jesus' name, amen!

# DAY 19

## Everyone Needs A Jonathan
## 1 Samuel 23:16

**Jonathan went to find David and encouraged him to stay strong in his faith in God.**

Everybody needs encouragement. Everybody needs someone that can pour into their lives and keep them going from time to time. It's good to be able to encourage yourself but it's even sweeter when someone else can add to it. Take a look at your inner circle and notate who are your Jonathans. If you don't find any in your circle, then let me assure you that is not healthy. You cannot be the only one encouraging in your circle. You cannot be the only one with pick-me-up words to say when the going gets tough. You cannot be the only one who everyone looks to for a positive word. That burden will soon break you. For your own emotional health please pray for God to reveal your Jonathans.

The life of David is one to be studied by all Christians. It is absolutely amazing. Jonathan was the son of Israel's first king, Saul. The moment these two got together they connected instantly. Even when Saul was seeking to kill David, Jonathan still held on to their friendship. The Bible states that their souls were as one. The relationship between Jonathan and David were so tight that Jonathan's father, the king, could not come between them. Jonathan recognized and respected the anointing on David's life which I can imagine made it easy for Jonathan to encourage him.

It is our duty as friends and even more so as Christians to encourage each other. Our encouragement may come in many ways. It may be a prayer, a hug, a card, a letter, cookies, a smile, a shoulder to cry on or just sitting in silence as support. We must make sure that we too have our Jonathans that can encourage us like we encourage others.

## Prayer

Father, I thank You for the gift of encouragement. Encouraging others brings me great joy and comfort. I realize that I too need to be encouraged from time to time. Please reveal to me who is my Jonathan. Open up my heart to receive from them. Fill them up with a word of encouragement just for me. I thank You for my Jonathans. In Jesus' name, amen!

# DAY 20

## Do You Know Who You Are?

## Exodus 1:15-21

¹⁵ Then Pharaoh, the king of Egypt, gave this order to the Hebrew midwives, Shiphrah and Puah: ¹⁶ "When you help the Hebrew women give birth, kill all the boys as soon as they are born. Allow only the baby girls to live." ¹⁷ But because the midwives feared God, they refused to obey the king and allowed the boys to live, too. ¹⁸ Then the king called for the midwives. "Why have you done this?" he demanded. "Why have you allowed the boys to live?" ¹⁹ "Sir," they told him, "the Hebrew women are very strong. They have their babies so quickly that we cannot get there in time!" They are not slow in giving birth like the Egyptian women." ²⁰ So God blessed the midwives, and the Israelites continued to multiply, growing more and more powerful. ²¹ And because the midwives feared God, he gave them families of their own.

Have you ever been in a situation when who you are conflicted with what to do? How do you handle it? Do you compromise and go along with the status quo or do you stand for who you are? Do you stay hidden in a closet wondering does anybody really know who I am? Does anybody care about who you really are? Do you know who you are?

We all have faced those challenges or will face them. Some of us didn't handle the situation the way we thought we would before getting into it. It's always easy to say what we will or won't do but for some reason when the situation actually arises and you have to make split second decisions, we sometimes do the opposite of what we thought we would do.

Afterwards, we are wondering what in the world just happened? The Hebrew midwives were told by the king of Egypt to do something that contradicted who they were and what they believed in. They chose to stand for who they were and not just go with the authority that was over them. That was bold! It's not always easy to stand up for your beliefs but it is a decision that we will have to make along this journey many times.

The pressures of this world are many and more people seek to be politically correct than right by God's standards. As Christians we have a duty and obligation to stand for what is right in spite of who it may be against. We cannot afford to waiver or be double minded (James 1:8). Our personality is what people perceive us to be but our character is who we really are.

## Prayer

Father, help me to realize my identity in You. Give me the strength and the boldness to stand for what is right on all occasions. I will allow Your word to be a lamp unto my feet and a light unto my path. My character shall never be in question because I shall always walk in integrity. My beliefs in You shall never be compromised. My values shall never be discredited because they come from studying Your word. I shall know where my identity lies. In Jesus' name, amen!

# DAY 21

## Are You an Original or a Carbon Copy?

### 2 Kings 17:15

**They rejected his laws and the covenant he had made with their ancestors, and they despised all his warnings. They worshiped worthless idols and became worthless themselves. They followed the example of the nations around them, disobeying the LORD's command not to imitate them.**

The Israelites were given specific instructions not to imitate other nations because those nations did not believe in God but instead worshipped idols. God had already made them into an original and He did not want them to become another carbon copy.

We live in a world where the media is telling women how to act, what to wear, where to go, what professions to be in, how to style your hair, how to raise your kids, what to eat, the best way to exercise, how to get a man, how to get rich, how to start a business and most importantly how to imitate the world. We have a lot of stuff being thrown at us to make us just another carbon copy.

You have to get to the point where you ask yourself, "Who am I imitating in this season? Who do I resemble the most? What does my heart reflect? How does it affect my thinking?"

You were never created to imitate anybody other than God. He is not surprised by the way you look. He is not caught off guard because of your past. He doesn't turn the other way when you mess up. So why are we trying to imitate everything and everyone but Him? Let us get back to doing what we were originally created to do. You don't know what that is? Then let me help you out. Just read the Bible. It has all the answers!

## Prayer

Father, I was created to imitate You and not this world. Help me to get back on track. I want my heart to imitate You. I want my thoughts to imitate You. I want my love to imitate You. I want my serving to imitate You. I want my giving to imitate You. I want my life to imitate You. I am an original and not another carbon copy of this world. My transformation is a work in progress and I won't give up until it is complete. In Jesus' name, amen!

# DAY 22

## Your Comfort Zone Won't Grow You

## Matthew 25:24-25

[24] "Then the servant with the one bag of gold came and said, 'Sir, I know you were a hard man, harvesting crops you didn't plant and gathering crops you didn't cultivate. [25] I was afraid I would lose your money, so I hid it in the earth and here it is.'

In this particular and familiar story a master was going away for a while and he left his servants in charge of different responsibilities based on what they could handle. There was one servant who only received one talent, which is translated into a certain sum of money. The other two servants were able to increase their talents and double what they were given but this servant hid his talent and did nothing.

Why would he hide it? Was he afraid that he would mess up? Did he not know who to use it? Was he just comfortable and decided no need for me to do anything extra? After all who likes to do a lot of extra work when you have so much to do already? What's wrong with doing the same thing all the time? It gives me the results I need and I can do it with my eyes closed. Does this sound familiar to anyone? I know that I am guilty.

If we never do anything new or different, then how do we grow? If we never step out of the box then how do we learn? If we never go outside the walls of our house then how do we meet new people? If we never challenge ourselves, then how do we know what we can handle? Sometimes the familiar can be a great hindrance to our growth without knowing it. Let's think about this for a minute.

There are numerous ways that we can step out of comfort zone and can cause growth in our lives in different areas. I challenge us to start now. Life is too short to be stuck in a rut. Live, Laugh and Love until your very last breath.

## Prayer

Father, help me to step out of my comfort zone so that I can grow in You. Holy Spirit, lead me in ways that I am hesitant in going. Show me what I'm missing. Sharpen my sight so that I can see the unseen. Broaden my understanding and increase my wisdom. In Jesus' name, amen.

# DAY 23

## Step Out of the Box
## John 8:36

**So if the Son sets you free, you will indeed be free.**

Don't allow people to put you in a box. You are too gifted for a box. You are too anointed for a box. You have too many talents for a box. Man cannot determine your reach. What does that mean? Man cannot choose when, where and how you can use what God has given you. Only God can give you limits.

Anyone who tries to isolate you, beware of them. If God has not confirmed it to you, then keep doing what you are doing. Sometimes people try to limit what they are not capable of doing, which leads to putting other people in boxes. You are too big to be in a box. Just because they can't see it doesn't mean that it can't be done. We walk by faith and not by sight. All things are possible with God. Everyday tell yourself that in the mirror.

It doesn't matter what it looks like in the natural. We have to speak those things that are not as if they were. Lazarus looked dead, but God. The woman with the issue of blood for 12 years appeared to be in a hopeless situation, but God. The man laying by the pool lame for 38 years looked as if that was his end, but God.

There is nothing too hard for our God. Step out of the box. Sometimes we put our own selves in a box because of fear or lack but today you can step out on faith. Who says that you can't do it? Who says that you can't achieve it? Who says that you don't have the qualifications? Who told you that you it was impossible? All you need is a "But God." I dare you to speak to your situation and declare, "But God!" I dare you to shout, "But God!" I dare you to praise on a, "But God."

## Prayer

Father, I am declaring my freedom today. I am free from every negative word that has been spoken over me. It shall not come to pass in Jesus' name. I am who God says I am. I am free from the stronghold that others are trying to put on my life. I am free from the nay-sayers. I am no longer bound by the box people have put me in. I'm breaking free today. I'm coming forth today. Greater is He that is in me than he that is in the world. I am declaring freedom from any and everything that is trying to steal, kill and destroy me! The anointing is breaking every yoke in my life right now. I am walking in Kingdom Authority! Hallelujah and Glory to God! Thank you Jesus for my freedom. In Jesus' name, amen!

# DAY 24

## Believe It and Don't Let It Go
## Genesis 39:19-23 NLT

**19 After hearing his wife's story, Potiphar was furious! 20 He took Joseph and threw him into the prison where the king's prisoners were held. 21 But the Lord was with Joseph there too, and he granted Joseph favor with the chief jailer. 22 Before long, the jailer put Joseph in charge of all the other prisoners and over everything that happened in the prison. 23 The chief jailer had no more worries after that, because Joseph took care of everything. The Lord was with him, making everything run smoothly and successfully.**

How many believers know that it's not over until God says so? Joseph just had a pit stop in life but it was never meant for him to stay there. His gift made room for him all the way to the palace of Pharaoh and positioned him to be able to bless his family in a time of need. (Proverbs 18:16)

Some of us have had pit stops in life but we are still there. Our pit stops were supposed to be a time of grooming and growing but instead we made it our life. We allowed our pit stop to devastate us and become our hindrance to reaching our God-given destiny. You still have the right and the power to come out of your pit. You can still walk in your Kingdom authority. You are still able to receive the victory after this. It's not too late. The end of your story has not been written yet. You may have been troubled but you are not in distress. You may have been perplexed but not in despair. This is your day and your season. You can still take back what the enemy thought he had control over. You can still stand tall and bold. You can still speak life while in the pit.

There's greater in you just looking for a way out. God can still cause you to succeed like never before. Tell that devil, "I'm coming out in the name of Jesus! I'm not your prisoner any longer. You can't hold me hostage any longer. I believe that I am the righteousness of God. You can't steal, kill and destroy my gifts any longer. You can no longer silence my voice or my praise. Greater is He that is in me than he that is in the world. I'm standing flat-footed on the promises of God. I shall have the victory! I'm going to believe it and not let it go."

## Prayer

Father, help me to believe I am what you see. In Jesus' name, amen!

# DAY 25

## Your Alarm Is Going Off

### Exodus 1:12

### But the more the Egyptians oppressed them, the more the Israelites multiplied! The Egyptians soon became alarmed

Just as the Egyptians became alarmed as the Israelites grew in number, in the same way the enemy gets alarmed when we grow spiritually. They become paranoid. They make it their sole purpose to steal, kill and destroy what God has for us. The Egyptians feared that the Israelites would rise up against them with their enemies and destroy them.

What has the enemy tried to destroy in your life? What has the enemy tried to discredit in your life? The enemy does not know our future but he does know that if we live by the word of God then we will come into the knowledge of the power that worketh in us (Ephesians 3:20). When it seems like the enemy is attacking you on every side it is because your alarm is going off. One of his workers told him that they saw you praying when they tried to attack you. Another worker reported that they saw you worshipping when you should have been crying. Another worker reported that your praise sent them straight back to hell. Then another reported that they tried to distract you but you were in the word of God. Your spiritual alarm is going off and he is trying to silence it.

The enemy is going to start with old tricks first to see if he can still get over on you. He's going to keep at it until he has silenced you by any means necessary. One thing he forgot is that this battle is not ours but the Lord's (2 Chronicles 20:15). Be encouraged; don't allow your process to discourage you from your destiny.

Listen beloved, the bottom line is this: the devil is afraid of your greatness. Don't allow him to suppress your greatness to mediocrity. We don't serve a mediocre God. We serve a Great God and He created us to be great!

## Prayer

Father, allow my greatness to come out for Your glory! The enemy will never silence or suppress me again. I now know that I am a threat to him. He is afraid of my spiritual alarm going off. I'm living out my God given purpose. I'm living out my God given assignment. I shall enjoy this life. I shall fight the good fight with faith and perseverance. I shall rise. I shall win in Jesus', amen!

# DAY 26

## The Chains Are Broken

## Ezekiel 18:1-4

**Then another message came to me from the Lord: 2 "Why do you quote this proverb concerning the land of Israel: 'The parents have eaten sour grapes, but their children's mouths pucker at the taste'? 3 As surely as I live, says the Sovereign Lord, you will not quote this proverb anymore in Israel. 4 For all people are mine to judge—both parents and children alike. And this is my rule: The person who sins will be the one who dies.**

In early Old Testament it was a given that the sins of the parents would be felt in the children. The life they lived was a preview of the lives of their children. But in this scripture that no longer suited God. He said the person who sins is the one who will die. In other words, the chains are broken. No longer would a child be hindered because of the sins of their parents.

You no longer have to walk around with the chains of your past. You no longer have to carry the chains of past hurt and mistakes. You no longer have to carry the chains of stress and depression. You no longer have to hold the chains of low self-esteem and negative body images. No, God has already broken those chains! Stop trying to reconnect what God has already destroyed! The cycle stops here.

God has broken every chain in your life that comes to steal, kill and destroy your purpose and destiny. The family curse is broken! It will not manifest in your life a second longer. Whatever negative words were spoken over your life has become null and void as of right now. Honey, don't wait until the storm is over. Shout now! The chain breaker has released you. The chain breaker has delivered you. The chain breaker has restored you. The chain breaker has revived you. The chain breaker is in your house. Do you hear the chains falling? Do you see the chains falling? Do you feel the chains falling? You are not bound anymore! You have been set free!

## Prayer

Father, I thank You for breaking my chains. These chains will no longer be my excuse in life but they have now become my testimony. I come boldly to let every demon in hell know that I will never be bound again. The chain breaker has released me so that I could help release somebody else. I see the chains falling. I hear the chains falling. Thank You God, for breaking every chain. In Jesus' mighty and powerful name, amen!

# DAY 27

## You Have Been Set Free
## 2 Corinthians 3:17

**Now, the Lord is the Spirit, and wherever the Spirit of the Lord is, he gives freedom.**

Freedom is the power or right to act, speak, or think as one wants without hindrance or restraint. As women a lot of restraints are put over us, therefore, hindering our growth in certain areas of our lives and leaving us unfulfilled. Women have had to fight for the same rights that were given to man from birth for a long time and some of us are still fighting that same battle.

There are women who are fighting against themselves because they can't get over what happened to them in their past. There are some who are unable to forgive themselves. There are women who have been defined by the words of others all their life but I just came to remind you that you are FREE!

You are FREE to love yourself. You are FREE to laugh out loud. You are FREE to live in peace and harmony. You are FREE from the bondage of your past. You are FREE to stand tall and bold. You are FREE to walk away from anything that is causing you pain. You are FREE to disconnect yourself from unhealthy relationships. You are FREE from that little box people have put you in for all these years that you didn't think that you would ever be able to come out. You are FREE to pursue your dreams. You are FREE to forgive and to love unconditionally.

Those who love with no fear will never be without love. My sister you are FREE! What are you going to do with your freedom?

## Prayer

Father, thank You for my freedom. I am free from my past. I am free from the hurt and pain caused by others. I am free from people trying to make me perfect. I am free from low self-esteem and depression. I am free from unhealthy relationships and people who are leeches in my life. Get thee behind me, Satan! I am walking in Kingdom Authority with this Fresh Wind! Satan you can't stop me because I'm free. Satan you can't block me because I'm free. Thank you Jesus for my freedom! I've been set free by the One who has all power of Heaven and earth in His hands. Hallelujah! In Jesus' name, amen!

# DAY 28

## But If Not

## Daniel 3:18

*"But even if he doesn't, Your Majesty can be sure that we will never serve your gods or worship the gold statue you have set up."*

How many of us need to tell the enemy, "BUT IF NOT?" I can imagine that you have been praying and fasting for a breakthrough for a while now and you may have become a little weary, but I dare you to tell the enemy, "BUT IF NOT!" Some of us are just believing God to do miracles in our lives in various areas but I challenge you to tell the enemy, "BUT IF NOT!" Your, "BUT IF NOT" is not a lack of faith or doubt. You are just reminding the enemy that even if God doesn't do it you are still not going to give up or give in.

"BUT IF NOT," Satan you are still a liar. "BUT IF NOT," Satan I'm not going to go with your plan. "BUT IF NOT," Satan I'm still going to serve and worship the only true and living God. "BUT IF NOT," Satan I'm still going to praise my God! We have to let the enemy know that our relationship with God is not conditional but everlasting! We have a real covenant with the Father.

Someone needs to shout, "BUT IF NOT!" Does anyone have a "BUT IF NOT" PRAISE IN THEIR HEART? God is still God, no matter how the situation ends.

## Prayer

Father, I believe that You will deliver me out of the hands of the enemy, but if not, let it be known that I will still serve only You. You are still the God of my life. You are still Alpha and Omega. You are still the Good Shepherd. You are the same God yesterday, today and forever more! You change not! Father, I have a praise in my heart just to confuse the enemy. I don't know how it's going to work out but I'm going to praise You anyhow. I don't know when it's going to work out but I'm going to praise You anyhow. I thank you Lord for my "but if not" praise! Hallelujah! In Jesus' name, amen!

# DAY 29

# It's Inventory Time

# Philippians 4:4

**Always be full of joy in the Lord. I say it again—rejoice!**

As I was getting ready to celebrate another year of life, the enemy started speaking to me. He began to tell me of all the things I don't have and what I have not accomplished. He began to account for some prayers that I'm still waiting on God to answer. He began to try and tell me that things are really not that good. He thought he had me but God…

Even though I'm still waiting, it's not what it looks like. I began to take an inventory over my life and these are some of the things that I found. I'm still alive and well! I may not be where I should be but I thank God I'm not where I use to be. My finances are not where I would like them but I don't have to beg for anything. I don't live in the house that I have dreamed of but I am able to keep a roof over my head. I am still be single but God has surrounded me with a lot of loving people. I am not the perfect parent but my child still walks in the favor of God! My career may not be where I want it but I'm blessed to be employed. As I look back over my life and think these things over, I can truly say that I am blessed. I am a living testimony!!!

You see, I had a choice. I could have given in to what the enemy was saying and threw myself a pity party and invited some folks to join in with me, but instead I chose to take inventory over my life and remind myself just how far God has brought me. He took a 15 year old teen mother with an attitude and chip on her shoulder and transformed her into a young woman who fears the Lord!

Yes, I'm still flawed with my own issues but I'm also blessed and highly favored! I'm a work in progress but I'm still filled with the Holy Spirit. I get weak sometimes but I still trust Him at His word!

When was the last time you took inventory over your life and proved the enemy wrong? Do it now for it is inventory time!

## Prayer

Father, thank You for this day that You have allowed me to see in spite of my shortcomings. Help me to take inventory over my life and remember all the things You have brought me through and delivered me. It's not what it looks like. I don't look like what I been through! My greater is coming! In Jesus' name, amen!

# DAY 30

## I Have the Victory
## 1 Corinthians 15:57

**How we thank God, who gives us victory over sin and death through Jesus Christ our Lord!**

To gain victory you have to defeat something or someone. Thanks be to God, we already have the victory before the battle ever started. We don't have to wish for victory. We don't have to dream for victory. The victory has already been won. We just have to remind ourselves from time to time, "I have the victory!"

When the devil tries to throw your past back in your face, declare, "I have the victory through Jesus Christ." When the boss tries to keep you from getting a promotion, declare, "I have the victory through Jesus Christ." When your enemies seem to increase, declare, "I have the victory through Jesus Christ." When the doctor gives you a bad report, declare, "I have the victory through Jesus Christ." When your character is being attacked, declare, "I have the victory through Jesus Christ."

In this declaration you are saying, Lord, however You give me the victory, I'm going to accept it. I put no limits on how this victory is going to manifest. I take my hands and my mouth off of it and give it to You. Do it, God, for Your glory! Do it, God, so men can praise You! Do it, God, and add to my testimony! Do it, God, and silence those who don't honor You! Do it, God, according to Your will.

## Prayer

Father, I thank You for my victories through Jesus Christ. I declare victory over every area of my life right now. I walk in victory through Jesus Christ. To God be the glory forever and ever. In Jesus' name, amen!

## Faith Confession

I am a woman in transformation for the glory of God

My mind is being renewed and my heart shall be pure (Matthew 5:6, Romans 12:2)

I shall present my body as a living sacrifice, holy and pleasing to God (Romans 12:1)

I shall have self-discipline and self-control

(1 Corinthians 9:24)

I shall live by the principles of God according to His word (Psalm 119:105)

I am a woman of worth (Psalm 139:14)

I am a woman of faith (2 Corinthians 5:7)

I walk in integrity and truth

(1 Samuel 12:24, Proverbs 8:7)

I am a woman in transformation for the glory of God

# ABOUT THE AUTHOR

Chantea M. Williams is a Christian writer, Bible teacher and speaker, who loves encouraging women to become greater through the word of God. Through her gifts, God created the Greater Working Women Ministries. They strive to encourage, empower and equip women from all walks of life to live out their God-given purpose with holy boldness. One of her many passions is baking, especially during the holidays. Don't miss her upcoming book for teen mothers entitled I Am Still Somebody coming in 2016. Sign up for our monthly newsletter at http://eepurl.com/k915. Also check out our Payhip store at http://payhip.com/gwwministry for other resources and free downloads.

Connect with Greater Working Women Ministries:
www.gwwministry.com
info@gwwministry.com
Facebook: gwwministry
Twitter: GreaterWomen
Pinterest: GWW Ministry
Instagram: gwwministry

Made in the USA
San Bernardino, CA
21 October 2015